Original title:
Leaves That Heal

Copyright © 2025 Creative Arts Management OÜ
All rights reserved.

Author: Aidan Marlowe
ISBN HARDBACK: 978-1-80581-910-3
ISBN PAPERBACK: 978-1-80581-437-5
ISBN EBOOK: 978-1-80581-910-3

Tuning the Heart with Nature

In the garden, whispers play,
Frogs croak tunes that sway.
Bees buzz with a silly song,
Flowers dance, all day long.

Worms wiggling, doing a jig,
Squirrels prance, not too big.
Nature's band, a quirky crew,
Jamming hard, making hearts new.

A breeze tickles my funny bone,
Trees giggle, never alone.
They share secrets, lost in chatter,
While butterflies debate what's better.

So here's to nature's hilarious flair,
A symphony beyond compare.
Tuning my heart to their wild beat,
With laughter and joy, life is sweet.

The Scent of Renewed Hope

Oh, the smell of morning dew,
It's like nature's perfume crew.
Dandelions in a fancy dress,
Telling worries to take a rest.

A squirrel slips on a nut—or two,
As I chuckle at their funny view.
The sun winks as it peeks through green,
Nature's jokes are the best I've seen.

Mushrooms plotting a party tonight,
With fairies dancing in moonlight.
A picnic of laughter and cheer,
Reminding us all that hope is near.

So let's savor laughter in the air,
Find joy in moments we all can share.
The scent of life, fresh and bold,
Is a story of hope that never gets old.

Reverberations of Renewal

In the garden, jokes take flight,
With plants that chuckle, pure delight.
A cactus winks with spiky cheer,
As daisies giggle, 'No need to fear!'

Ferns burst forth with leafy grins,
While sunflowers tease with their wins.
In whispers soft, the petals speak,
Of comic tales they like to peek.

Repose in Rustic Green

Under an oak, I lay my head,
It cracks a joke, it's well-read.
The willow whispers funny tales,
As breezes dance with leafy trails.

A squirrel up high begins to prance,
While branches sway, they join the dance.
"More nuts!" he shouts, with laughter bold,
As acorns drop, like tales retold.

Topiary Tranquility

Bushes shaped like funny clowns,
Sit amidst the giggling towns.
A hedgehog laughs, it's quite a sight,
As sculpted greens bring sheer delight.

The bushes chat, they twist and turn,
"Let's hold a party!" they all yearn.
With laughter sprouting all around,
In this green space, joy's profound.

The Golden Touch of Green

A golden leaf with flair and sheen,
Claims it's the king, so bold, so green.
"The sun is mine!" he beams with pride,
As butterflies float and swirl beside.

"Let's throw a bash, come one, come all!"
The bright ones answer to the call.
In joy we'll bask, and wink away,
As nature's fun is here to stay!

Secrets of the Understory

Among the ferns, the whispers play,
Sassy little critters joke all day.
A mushroom's cap, a tiny hat,
"I'm king of the forest!"—oh, how they chat.

Squirrels flirt with acorns, quite the romance,
While roots below throw a wild dance.
In shadows, laughter tickles the breeze,
Nature's jesters, just aim to please.

Canopy of Calm

Up high in branches, giggles entwine,
With every gust, leaves sway and whine.
"Hold on tight!" chirp birds in flight,
As they dive into clouds, what a silly sight!

A raccoon spins tales of nighttime snacks,
He insists they're better than a fish's hacks.
Underneath stars, they twinkle and gleam,
"Who needs a blanket when you've got a dream?"

Green Refuge: A Solace

In a secret nook, the vines are loose,
They whisper gossip of the neighborhood moose.
"Did you see his dance? What a curious sight!"
Said the daisies giggling, blooming so bright.

Butterflies munch on pollen-flavored cake,
While ants plot a picnic by the big lake.
"Oh dear, they're coming!" frogs croak with a leap,
"Let's hide in the marsh where it's safe, and it's deep!"

Breaths of the Wild

In each soft rustle, a chuckle is found,
A squirrel spills secrets, all around.
"Who stole my acorn?!" cries the nutty thief,
As owls rotate heads, pondering the grief.

Branches sway low, like a hippy's groove,
Nature's own disco, come join the move!
With mossy seats and a sunbeam light,
Here's the place where laughter feels right.

Banishing the Storm

When clouds roll in and skies turn gray,
I grab my coat and run away.
But find a shrub that grins, oh dear,
And suddenly, I've lost my fear!

Its leaves shout loud, a comic flare,
Dancing 'round without a care.
I skip and jump, the storm will wait,
For nature's giggle seals my fate!

Wildflower Dreams

In fields of bright, a daisy schemes,
To tickle toes and stir up dreams.
A butterfly's a jokester bold,
With stories of a world untold.

They whisper secrets, oh so sly,
From petals bright to soaring high.
A wild parade of joyful cheer,
Who knew that fluff made laughter near?

Echoes from the Green Heart

The trees all chuckle, branches sway,
As squirrels host a circus play.
They juggle acorns, tails in loops,
While mossy benches share the scoops!

With every rustle comes a joke,
Like nature's breath, it's all bespoke.
In symphonies of rustling green,
The best-kept secrets still unseen!

Sanctuary of the Verdant

In emerald halls where laughter blooms,
I found a chair among the plumes.
A hedgehog, wise, with quills so fine,
Serves tea, while mushrooms sip on wine.

The ferns retell the tales of dirt,
And every whispered word won't hurt.
Where giggles grow and shadows play,
I'm lost in joy and bright bouquet!

Mending under the Moonlit Leaves

When the nightlight glimmers bright,
Beneath the branches, what a sight!
We patch our hearts with laughter loud,
And twirl like children, joyful, proud.

The owls are hooting, joining in,
With wise old winks and silly grins,
We stitch our woes with silly threads,
And dance around like playful beds.

In shadows deep, we find our cheer,
With every chuckle, doubts disappear.
The moon is watching, winking too,
A leafy patchwork, just for you!

So gather 'round this silly spot,
Where every giggle unknots the knot.
As nature whispers secrets sweet,
We mend our hearts with joyful beat.

Renewal in the Breeze

A gust of wind, a funny tease,
Whirls around like a playful sneeze.
It tickles noses, flips our hats,
While nature chuckles, how it spats!

The flowers giggle, sway around,
As bees buzz softly, not a sound.
We leap alongside with silly glee,
Getting tangled in a leaf spree.

Even the grass gets in on fun,
Whispering secrets in the sun.
We kick up dirt with silly shouts,
Finding joy in all those clouts!

So as we wander 'neath the trees,
Let's welcome change on playful knees.
With every breath, we twist and sway,
Renew our spirits, come what may.

Greened Pathways of Breathe

On trails adorned with emerald hues,
We walk with giggles, share our views.
The leaves above dance in delight,
As we prance onward, out of sight.

Each step a skip, a funny fall,
Who knew a stroll could be this small?
With every breath, we share a smile,
Making memories, mile by mile.

A squirrel darts by, oh what a rush,
Chasing its tail, in silly hush.
We laugh aloud while hopping high,
As butterflies swirl in the sky.

So come with me, let joy unfold,
On pathways green and stories told.
We'll breathe in life and laugh it through,
In this wild world, just me and you.

The Quiet Resurgence

In the stillness, whispers arise,
As nature plots with tiny sighs.
The petals curl in goofy ways,
Winking at us through dreamy haze.

Soft rustles tease our listening ears,
Each giggle muffled, lost in cheers.
A patchwork quilt of vibrant spread,
We tiptoe upon what's left unsaid.

Amidst the hush, oh what a jest,
We find our peace and comic rest.
With every breeze, a chuckle tight,
We gather joy as day turns night.

So let's embrace the gentle sway,
And dance in whispers of the day.
With quiet hearts, we rise anew,
In laughter's warmth, just me and you.

The Healing Hand of Nature

In a garden filled with laughter,
A weed wore a happy hat.
Doctors said to take it easy,
But no one mentioned a chat.

Chasing butterflies for healing,
They giggled as they flew.
A tickle from the dandelions,
Made them sneeze, "Achoo!"

Bumblebees bounced like dancers,
On blossoms bright and gay.
Nature's hugs were contagious,
In a comical ballet.

So if you're feeling down, my friend,
Just find a patch of cheer.
The hand of nature works quite well,
With laughter in the air!

Sacred Green Spaces

In parks where squirrels hold meetings,
They plot their daily pranks.
The trees nod in silent wisdom,
As nature gives them thanks.

A patch of grass was softly singing,
With worms as backup crew.
They serenaded passing joggers,
That slipped in morning dew.

The flowers wore their brightest colors,
In a runway fit for dreams.
Their petals laughed in the sunshine,
And danced in playful streams.

So seek those sacred green spaces,
Where joy grows evergreen.
Even the weeds join the laughter,
In nature's comical scene!

Refreshing Tides of the Wild

A river chuckled past the rocks,
Telling tales of fishy tricks.
"Try swimming upstream!" it said,
"It's where the fun really clicks!"

Tall grasses waved their leafy hands,
With splashes of fresh sass.
They teased the frogs, who leaped for joy,
In a splashy, wild ballet class.

The sunbeams winked at sneaky ants,
Who marched in silly lines.
Together they formed a dance brigade,
To nature's light-filled signs.

So if you seek refreshing tides,
Find laughter in the wild.
Nature's giggles are contagious,
And leave you feeling wild!

Nestled in Nature's Grasp

In the forest, whispers giggle,
As branches sway and sway.
A fox tells tales with fuzzy ears,
While the bees buzz in ballet.

Cozy shadows hold secrets tight,
With mushrooms sharing tea.
Squirrels hop from branch to branch,
With jokes planted on every tree.

The brook sings softly, a bubbly voice,
While critters laugh and play.
While leaves in harmony shimmy down,
And giggle their own way.

So if you're feeling rather grim,
Find a nook where nature laughs.
Nestled in nature's warm embrace,
You'll find joy in all its drafts.

Cradle of the Forest

In the woods where critters play,
Tiny nudges make them sway.
A leaf whispered to a bug,
"Can I give your back a hug?"

Bouncing high, a squirrel grinned,
He just knew he'd always win.
With acorns tossed like little snacks,
He danced around in silly tracks.

The trees chuckled in their gowns,
While the mushrooms spun in crowns.
"Oh, come and join the fun!" they said,
As splashes of green danced overhead.

A breeze brought giggles, oh so sweet,
Twirling all around their feet.
In this cradle, wild yet fun,
Nature's joy has just begun!

The Lullaby of Flora

In the garden where flowers snooze,
A daisy whispered, "What's the news?"
"I've heard the roses snore like bears,
They'll wake up soon, so bring your chairs!"

A bumblebee buzzed, all in a whirl,
"Did you spot the dandelion girl?"
"She's fluffing up and spreading cheer,
With seeds that fly — oh dear, oh dear!"

The tulips danced, in perfect rows,
Turning shy when the bluebird chose.
"Hey there, sprout! You can't hide long,
Napping here isn't your real song!"

Lullabies hummed through the night,
Every bud was waking right.
With gentle jokes, the petals spun,
In laughter's bloom, they had their fun!

Nature's Touch of Solace

A willow waved, all soft and grand,
"Come take a break, it's quite unplanned!"
A rabbit flopped, and said, "Oh sure,
Let's make some tea — I'll bring the cure!"

A hedgehog rolled from side to side,
With prickles up, he took a ride.
"Just don't spill — it's quite a mess!"
The others laughed, it's all a jest.

Herbs were chatting, full of sass,
"A little mint might bring some class!"
Thyme chimed in, with witty flair,
"Just watch where you breathe, it's everywhere!"

In golden rays, they felt so fine,
Nature's blessings, oh divine.
In this funny, cozy nook,
They shared their tales — just take a look!

Petals of Restoration

In the meadow, laughter bloomed,
Where butterflies giggled and twirled in gloom.
"What's that? A tulip with a hat?"
Daydreaming flowers said, "What's up with that?"

A clover leapt, with four leaves tight,
"I'm feeling lucky, what a sight!"
But stumbled over, with a snicker loud,
"It's tough to run when you're so proud!"

The sunflowers waved, tall like a tower,
Racing the wind, oh what power!
"Who's faster? The breeze or me?"
Laughter echoed, "Wait and see!"

In whimsical games, the petals talked,
Underneath where the daisies walked.
A garden filled with joy and glee,
Nature's humor, wild and free!

The Healing Greenway

In a park where laughter flows,
Pickles dance where the green grass grows.
A squirrel wearing a tiny hat,
Judges who's more stylish than a cat.

A breeze whispers secrets to trees,
As flowers gossip, swaying with ease.
A trampoline made of soft green leaves,
Where everyone bounces and nobody grieves.

Flora's Gentle Cure

In a garden where giggles grow,
Herbs tell jokes and put on a show.
Rosemary cracks puns about thyme,
As daisies dance — oh, isn't it prime?

The minty refreshment, a sprightly cheer,
Tickling your nose, it whispers near.
And honeybees hum a merry tune,
Beware of mosquitoes, they'll swoon at noon!

Renewal in the Wilderness

Out in the wild where the critters roam,
Even a bear feels like he's at home.
A raccoon steals snacks with a cheeky grin,
While frogs throw a party with their violin.

Plants wear pajamas made of bright hue,
Dancing in moonlight, as stars bid adieu.
Laughter echoes 'round each winding trail,
Even the pine trees chuckle and hail!

Nature's Quiet Release

In the woods where the sunlight pranks,
Bushes burst out with their funny ranks.
Mushrooms giggle beneath tall pines,
As clouds trip over, spilling their lines.

A rabbit strikes poses, being quite grand,
While turtles slow dance — isn't life bland?
With each gentle flutter, a joke's in the air,
Nature's delight — a funny affair!

Sanctuary in the Shade

Under branches lush and wide,
A squirrel danced, almost fried.
He slipped on acorns, what a sight!
The sun was hot, he took to flight.

In the shade, the daisies yawn,
While bumblebees buzz sing their song.
A picnic spread on grassy floor,
With ants that steal the chips, for sure!

A bird fluffs up and starts to chirp,
As children giggle, toss and burp.
The tree just shakes its leafy head,
'This place is magic, just like bread!'

But if you wander far, beware,
For spiders might just give a scare.
Yet laughter lingers in the air,
In this green hideaway where we dare.

Echoes of Evergreen Comfort

In the forest, not a sound,
Except for laughter spinning round.
A deer jogs in her finest flair,
While chipmunks cling with shiny hair.

The pines are swaying, what a scene!
A raccoon pops up, all so keen.
He checks the snacks we've laid around,
And snickers softly, not a sound.

Upon the branches, squirrels chat,
They plot and scheme, just like a cat.
With little paws and tiny grace,
In this green realm, they set the pace.

A gust of wind, a playful tease,
Up goes a hat, into the trees!
But here in shade, we're all at ease,
In evergreen comfort, joys like these.

Whispers of Nature's Embrace

Beneath a giant, leafy dome,
A fox prances, finding home.
He shuffles past the picnic spread,
While ants conspire, dreams in their head.

Among the trees, a wise owl hoots,
As everyone munches on fabulous fruits.
The laughter bounces, the giggles soar,
All in love with the great outdoors.

A butterfly flits, oh what a show,
It dances wildly, here and there it goes.
And in the shade, the fun won't cease,
With nature's whispers granting peace.

They tease and play, they roll around,
While nature giggles, what a sound!
In this embrace, we find our cheer,
With every moment, joy's so near!

Balm in the Canopy

Up high, the branches flitter and sway,
While hidden critters weave their play.
A bashful turtle pokes her head,
In dreams of sunshine, she's well-fed.

A friendly spider spins her thread,
Her web a hammock, laid out ahead.
With laughter echoing all around,
In this green balm, joy is found.

The birds hold court, a lively choir,
Their tunes a mix of fun and fire.
A lizard joins, he's got some moves,
In this leafy room, everyone grooves.

But watch out now, for sudden drops,
Of acorns, pinecones—don't lose your crops!
Still laughter lingers in the air,
In this fun sanctuary, we all share!

Renewal Beneath the Canopy

In a forest where giggles grow,
Squirrels dance, putting on a show.
Trees wear hats of leafy green,
Fashion trends quite rarely seen.

Beneath the branches, critters play,
Exchanging jokes throughout the day.
Frogs croak laughter, birds take flight,
Under the canopy, pure delight.

Worms do yoga, stretching slow,
While trees gossip, row by row.
Nature's charm wraps snug and tight,
Creating joy, oh what a sight!

A breeze whispers a silly tune,
As rabbits prance beneath the moon.
With every rustle, a chuckle's shared,
In this place, no heart is spared.

A Path of Verdant Grace

Along a path where greens collide,
Tiny ants march side by side.
They're carrying crumbs, oh what a feat,
In this leafy world, they own the street.

A plushy moss breaks out in song,
With a beat that feels just right or wrong.
The trees sway, they're quite the crowd,
Cracking jokes, feeling bold and proud.

Magpies steal the show with style,
Dressed in black that makes us smile.
Their flashy moves are quite a sight,
Who knew birds could dance all night?

In the grass, the snails race fast,
Pacing slow, they're unsurpassed.
No better way to greet the day,
On this path where fun will play.

Arboreal Healing

In a glade where shadows bounce,
Bouncing boars do quite the pounce.
Raccoons laugh, they find it grand,
To play a tune with sticks in hand.

A tree with bark of polka dots,
Offers shade, and ties lots of knots.
Squirrels confide their gossip bold,
In tales of acorns turned to gold.

The ferns do a wiggly dance,
While beetles roll like they're in a trance.
Nature's humor reigns supreme,
In this forest, laughter beams.

The owls hoot in comic rhythm,
While squirrels plot a funny schism.
In this realm where chuckles thrive,
Every creature feels alive.

The Solace of Braided Branches

Under branches, laughter swells,
With every tale that nature tells.
Chipmunks scamper with a grin,
As shadows hide the mischief within.

The branches twist in playful knots,
Hosting parties for all the tots.
Each breeze brings a tickling tease,
As Bumblebees buzz with such ease.

A wise old tree with a beard so long,
Whispers secrets in a voice that's strong.
The vines laugh back, they quip and quirk,
Their leafy jokes, a whimsical work.

In this sanctuary of leafy jest,
Every heart can find its rest.
For nature's laughter, loud and clear,
Fills our souls with endless cheer.

Whispers of the Emerald Canopy

In the garden, a squirrel did prance,
Hiding treasures, taking a chance.
With an acorn so large, it tipped on its head,
Chasing sunbeams, where the spices are spread.

A leaf tickled my nose, gave me a fright,
I laughed so hard, almost took flight.
It danced in the breeze, with a giggle and glee,
Like a jester on stage, just amusing for me.

Nature's Tender Touch

A dandelion puff blew past with flair,
In my hair, a new style, quite rare.
With a frizzy wild look, I struck a pose,
Nature's new trend—who knew, I suppose?

The grass sang a tune underfoot with cheer,
Tapping my toes, the rhythm was clear.
With each little step, the earth played along,
In this wacky concert, I felt just like a song!

The Green Embrace

In autumn's parade, colors come alive,
But I tripped on a twirl—oh, how I thrive!
A bright yellow leaf, now stuck to my shoe,
Reminding me daily, it's funny what's true.

A round little frog croaked an old joke,
While a ladybug laughed, or maybe it spoke.
Nature's own comedy—what a delight,
Turning fallen leaves into pure joy and light.

Fragments of Renewal

A tiny sprout peeking out from the ground,
Said, "Hey there, friend! Come play, don't you frown!"
With roots like spaghetti, it wobbled just so,
Declaring a party—come on, don't be slow!

Caterpillars joined, with suits all askew,
Wearing their stripes, they danced in a queue.
Nature's own circus, a show that won't end,
Where laughter and giggles are always on the mend!

Forest's Embrace

In the woods, a squirrel sneezed,
A nut flew far, his aim just teased.
The branches laughed, they danced and swayed,
As nature's jokes were deftly played.

A deer asked birds for fashion tips,
They showed her trends and fancy flips.
With style so fresh and grace so sweet,
She pranced around on dainty feet.

A turtle joined the joyful scene,
With a leaf hat, he felt like a queen!
But when it rained, oh what a sight,
He slipped and slid, oh what a fright!

The forest chuckled, trees stood tall,
Nature's humor, it had a ball.
With giggles echoing through each glade,
In this green haven, joy was made.

Healing under the Boughs

A rabbit sat with tea in paw,
Complaining loudly, 'Oh, the raw!
My carrot stash was swiped by crows!'
The boughs just giggled as he dozed.

A hedgehog brought a tiny chair,
He filled it up with thorny flair.
'Just sit and chill, my friend,' he said,
'Forget your woes, life's better fed!'

An owl named Hoot gave sage advice,
'Just crack a joke, it'll suffice!'
They laughed until the stars took flight,
In this green nook, all felt just right.

With plushy moss as comfy beds,
The laughter twinkled in their heads.
All under branches, soft and fine,
In nature's laughter, they'd entwine.

Verdant Whispers of Relief

In the shade, a chipmunk grinned,
'I've lost my way, but found a friend!'
They danced on grass, with flower crowns,
Comedy boots there, were quite the clowns.

A frog leapt high, but then he missed,
And landed right in nature's mist!
Giggles rose from creatures small,
As ripples cast a giggling thrall.

The foxes played a game of tag,
But tripped on roots, oh what a drag!
They flipped and flopped and rolled about,
In muddy joy, without a doubt.

The whispers rustled, secrets shared,
Of funny moments, never spared.
In shades of green, they held their glee,
For laughter's roots run deep and free.

Serene Shadows and Comfort

In shadowed nooks, a bear reclined,
With honey dreams, and thoughts entwined.
He snored so loud, the birds took flight,
'This guy's a riot!', they chirped in fright.

A misfit porcupine, quite spry,
Wore sunglasses while passing by.
He struck a pose, 'I'm very cool!'
Nature laughed at this leafy fool.

A picnic spread so wide and grand,
With ants that marched, a marching band.
But when they feasted, oh what a sight,
They spilled the jam, what pure delight!

The sun peeped through, as shadows danced,
In nature's arms, they all romanced.
With giggles shared and joy replete,
In serene embrace, they found their beat.

A Symphony of Soothe

In the garden, confusion sows,
Tickling toes where the wild grass grows.
Swaying softly, the blooms do dance,
Whispering secrets of a sunlit trance.

Bumblebees buzzing, don't mind the noise,
They're the band playing with cheerful poise.
Each petal a note, each stem a beat,
Even the weeds join in, isn't that neat?

The daisies wear shades, so cool and bright,
While clovers conspire from morning to night.
Laughter erupts from branches so wide,
As creatures convene for a friendly ride.

So let's raise a glass to this leafy spree,
With roots deep in joy, we'll all be carefree.
In this wild concert, we'll find our groove,
With each little giggle, we'll just keep moving!

The Sprout of Comfort

A sprout peeks up in a curious way,
Waving at clouds as they float and play.
It tickles the tummy, oh such delight,
Naturally bright in the warm sunlight!

Bananas in pajamas swing from above,
A chatty chipmunk finds a nut to love.
Every new shoot, a comical sight,
Reminds us of joy with each morning light.

Giggling squirrels in leafy attire,
Hold secret meetings to share their desire.
To tickle one another with little acorns,
While crafting a plan for their fluffy fawns.

A festival sprouting with laughter and cheer,
With each simple moment, we draw them near.
So let's dance with sprouts, oh what a thrill,
In a world full of giggles, our hearts will fill!

Essence of the Enchanted Grove

In the grove where the silliness flows,
Trees sport hats in whimsical rows.
A picnic of giggles, a buffet of glee,
Where even the moss sings, "Come dance with me!"

Toadstools in clusters, a colorful crew,
They've planned a tea party for me and you.
With cookies from clovers and juice from the rain,
They'll serve up laughter, it's never mundane!

Whimsical winks sway with every breeze,
As shadows play tag and the sun takes its ease.
For every bark giggles and whispers so light,
Join in the fun—it's a pure-hearted sight!

With fairies on swings and the wind as a song,
This enchanted escape, where all can belong.
Let's gather our wishes and toss them in air,
In this grove of delight, we've nothing to spare!

Breezes of Rejuvenation

A breeze with a snicker runs over the glade,
Tickling flowers that bask in the shade.
"Oh do feel the curls in my hair!" it pleads,
As laughter erupts from the tickled seeds!

Caterpillars giggle, all fuzzy and slow,
Competing in races, look at them go!
With each twist and turn, they roll on the grass,
Chasing their friends, oh what a classy mass!

Sunbeams pop in like a joke on the run,
Finding the punchlines to tickle the sun.
"Why do cows jump over the moon?" they tease,
Sharing old tales on the soft summer breeze.

With flowers all smiling, and laughter in air,
Let's take a deep breath, forgetting our care.
In the dance of the breezes, our spirits will soar,
Renewed by the giggles, who could ask for more?

Nature's Soft Caress

In the park, a squirrel prances,
Grabbing snacks with wild glances.
A twig snaps, and now he's off,
While birds laugh with a cheerful scoff.

Beneath the shade, a nap I take,
Waking up to a laughing lake.
The frogs croak out a melody,
While turtles chill in tranquility.

A breeze tickles, I start to sneeze,
But with each sneeze, I catch a breeze.
Nature's joke is quite severe,
Making me laugh and shed a tear.

A grasshopper jumps, a sudden twist,
Attacking my sandwich, oh, how it missed!
Nature's whimsy, a playful tease,
In the park, I lose all my unease.

The Healing Canopy

Under the trees, I spot a cat,
Wearing a hat, imagine that!
He struts around with such a flair,
Claiming this shade as his own lair.

The wind whispers sweet nothings low,
While ants line up for a toe-to-toe.
A ladybug rolls in a funny way,
As if to join in on the play.

The sun peeks through, a game of hides,
While butterflies do silly slide.
Bouncing flowers nod, all agree,
Nature's giggles belong to me!

A fungi pops up with a cheeky grin,
Making me wonder where it's been.
In this lush world where jesters thrive,
I find my joy, I feel alive!

Symphony of Flora

A bloom winks, it's quite a flirt,
While bees buzz by in their little shirt.
Dancing daisies down the lane,
A rainbow bright, oh, how they reign!

A dandelion gives a mighty blow,
Sending seeds out to the show.
With poof! Poof! All around the spot,
Its dance is wild; is it too hot?

The willow sways with a spirit free,
Knocking hats off folks like me.
Nature's concert, a funny scene,
With each note played by the unseen.

A rose exclaims with all its might,
"I've got thorns, but I'm still a delight!"
In laughter's sway, I find my calm,
In nature's play, there's a gentle balm.

Embraced by Green

In a meadow filled with soft delight,
A goat joins in the verbal fight.
With bleats and jumps, he steals the show,
While grass tickles his chin, oh so slow!

A frisbee flies; a dog runs fast,
He misses it—oh, what a blast!
He trips on a root and does a roll,
Grass stains laughing, heart and soul.

Cats and dogs in a leafy maze,
Squirrels plotting their nutty craze.
With giggles echoing high and low,
Nature sets the mood for a go-go show!

So let us dance in this green embrace,
Where joy finds a most charming space.
With nature's humor, we'll always feel,
The softest laughs that truly heal.

Songs of the Verdant

In a garden glee, where the laughter grows,
A cabbage once danced, in farmer's old clothes.
It pranced with potatoes, a veggie ballet,
While chives played the lute, in a green cabaret.

The flowers were jesters, with petals in tow,
Telling tall tales of the sun's golden glow.
Bees buzzed with humor, their jokes on the wing,
In a world full of chuckles, where green hearts sing.

Amidst this wild madness, a broccoli king,
Proclaimed every brussels sprout's right to swing.
With carrots as dancers, in a jazzy parade,
The rhythm of nature was perfectly made.

So let's raise a toast, to the harvest we share,
To the laughter of gardens beyond compare.
For in every bouquet, there's a pun to be spun,
In the songs of the verdant, we're all full of fun!

Nature's Gentle Remedy

A dandelion doctor, with glasses askew,
Sent patients on hikes, for a refreshing view.
"Just breathe in the green, let your worries take flight,
And hop like a bunny, till you feel just right!"

Beneath the tall oaks, a wise turtle would grin,
He offered free naps, for a moment to win.
"Just trust in the grass, let your dreams start to flow,
And wake up with giggles, our special 'whoa!'"

The violets chuckled, they made quite a fuss,
Telling wild stories without any fuss.
A thistle chimed in, "Oh, life's like a joke,
We're all part of laughter, till the last croak!"

So take a good stroll, feel the joy in your soul,
Let nature's fine humor make you feel whole.
With every green whisper, and each tiny cheer,
It's simply a remedy, that brings us near!

Echoes of Green Serenity

In a meadow of mirth, where the daisies all giggle,
A mullein made muffins, with a sly little wiggle.
"Come feast on my treats, they're filled with delight,
A sprinkle of sunshine, they're fluffy and light!"

The willows would whisper, with secrets so fine,
"Why did the fern cross? To get to the vine!"
With laughter that echoed, through valleys and glades,
The tongue-in-cheek humor cascaded like shades.

A hedgehog in spectacles, reading the news,
Declared "Every leaf thinks it's got the best views!"
With jokes from the lilies, and puns from the ferns,
The green serenade taught us all about turns.

So dance with the daisies and twirl with the breeze,
Remember that laughter can help us with ease.
In echoes of green, there's a truth to be found,
A joy that unites, in this whimsical ground!

Tapestry of Renewal

In the quilt of the woodlands, each thread tells a tale,
Of squirrels with acorns, and raccoons who sail.
With stitches of laughter, and patches of cheer,
Of chipmunks who giggle, as winter draws near.

A robin once painted, his nest with a brush,
Declared "I'm an artist, in the morning rush!"
With worms as his muse, he chirped through the day,
In a symphony silly, where clouds liked to play.

The shrubs held a soiree, for critters so sly,
To sip on sweet nectar and share a good pie.
The ants brought their humor, the frogs croaked a tune,
While foxes pirouetted, 'neath the light of the moon.

So weave in the chuckles, let nature entwine,
In this lively dance, where all hearts align.
With joy as our fabric, let's gather the fun,
A tapestry woven, where laughter has won!

Growth in Softness

In gardens bright, the plants conspire,
To grow real tall, like liars in a choir.
They stretch and bend with a goofy grace,
While squirrels play tag in a leafy race.

Sunlight tickles the seeds below,
Making them giggle as they start to grow.
A cactus couldn't care less, it's proud,
While daisies blow kisses for the crowd.

Roots do the cha-cha under the ground,
In earthy disco, where joy abounds.
Nature's nonsense, it's hard to deem,
But somewhere in chaos, there's always a dream.

Petals in the Wind

Petals float like silly hats,
Drifting down like cheerful cats.
They spin and twirl on breezy swings,
Performing tricks like circus kings.

Dandelions giggle as they take flight,
Making wishes under moonlight.
The tulips chuckle with colors so bright,
As bees wear goggles to fly at night.

A butterfly jokes, 'I'm off to the fair!'
With wings like laughter, it fills the air.
The garden's a stage, where all take part,
In a dance of nature, a whimsical art.

The Healing Torrent of Green

In a jungle, trees plot the next big trend,
Where vines play games and roots pretend.
Ferns start a rumor, it's quite absurd,
That they're the stars—have you heard?

Rain dribbles down like a playful scene,
Making puddles for frogs to convene.
The moss wears a blanket, so cozy and neat,
While snails in their shells shuffle their feet.

A river giggles, singing a song,
As grasshoppers dance, or maybe they prong.
With nature's orchestra hitting the tune,
It celebrates life on a wild afternoon!

Under the Arch of Life

Beneath the trees, where shadows play,
The ants throw a party at the end of the day.
With crumbs for a feast, it's quite the delight,
While beetles roll snacks in the fading light.

The arch above hums a gentle tune,
As crickets chirp to a brightening moon.
Squirrels audition for their comedy role,
With acorns galore, they're on a stroll.

Branches sway as if telling a joke,
While butterflies giggle and slowly poke.
In this wild theater, life takes a chance,
Under the arch, every leaf joins the dance.

Choreography of Change

In the autumn dance, they twirl with ease,
Dropping off branches like sneezes in breeze.
A pirouette here, a shiver there,
They shimmy and shake without a care.

Nature's ballet makes us chuckle and smile,
With a rustle of giggles, they prance for a while.
In twirls of orange, they look quite absurd,
Like gymnasts in action, without a word.

As winter approaches, they'll perform a slight dip,
Falling and fluttering, they never lose grip.
Oh, the fun watching them perform in the air,
Their winding routine without a single scare!

So here's to the leaves in their curious plight,
Their harvest of joy is a wonderful sight.
With each swirling drop, they spread out their cheer,
In the show of the seasons, they're the stars here!

Colors of Restoration

Dancing in sunlight, their colors so bright,
They wear shades of laughter, pure delight.
From emerald to amber with a twinkling glee,
Like a rainbow's remark, oh, what a spree!

Some wear a hat of red, so absurd,
While others play dress-up with outfits unheard.
They flop and they flutter in all of their hues,
Creating a canvas, they've got nothing to lose.

With whispers of change in the wondrous air,
They paint back the smiles, unravel despair.
Like a jester's parade in an ever-twirling show,
These colorful wonders, steal the whole show!

So here's to the colors that come and that fade,
In the wacky realm of a fun masquerade.
With every new season, they start something new,
In the dance of hilarity, they know what to do!

Tapestry of Renewal

Woven in laughter, the tapestry shines,
With threads of good humor and playful designs.
It's a patchwork of giggles in a whimsical hue,
Stitched with the secrets the seasons imbue.

Each square a memory, a quirky delight,
A frayed edge of wisdom, the fun takes flight.
They weave through the forest, a jolly parade,
Creating a quilt with the joy of their trade.

Their patterns are laughter, their colors a cheer,
In a whirlwind of whimsy, they conquer the year.
With a thread made of sunshine, they playfully dwell,
In the fabric of nature, where all is so swell!

So let's raise a toast to this tapestry grand,
With a wink and a nod, as we take a stand.
For the art of the dance in this colorful reel,
Is a whimsical vision that's perfectly real!

Vitality in Variegation

Oh, the vibrant show of those chaotic hues,
A party of patterns that banish the blues.
Like a circus of patches where fun's all around,
With a wink from the sun, they make joy abound!

Each variant a giggle, each spot a delight,
A plaid of the playful in morning's first light.
They burst from the branches like confetti galore,
A festival dressed in the fun they explore.

With stripes and with splotches, they strut with such flair,

The giggling greens flaunt what's beyond compare.
In a dash of fresh laughter, they find their own beat,
Spinning tales of mirth in a playful retreat.

So here's to the vitality, the whirl and the swirl,
Of nature's own confetti in a delightful whirl.
In variegated glory, they spread out their cheer,
In a world full of chuckles, there's nothing to fear!

Miracles of the Meadow

In the meadow where wild things play,
Grass tickles our toes all day.
Butterflies dance, doing the cha-cha,
While rabbits munch on their okra.

Squirrels gossip, with acorn hats,
Telling tales of their feathered chats.
Bumblebees buzz in silly circles,
While frogs croak jokes, looking like miracles.

Dandelions sprout with a wink,
Spreading their fluff, making us think.
Every flower takes a bow,
As if to say, "Look at me now!"

Oh, the laugh of nature's jest,
Each plant plays its role, they're the best!
In this merry green parade,
We find joy that will never fade.

Regeneration in Rustling Hues

Colors everywhere, splashed with cheer,
Nature's palette makes us revere.
Golden sunlight, like a hooded cape,
Makes the grass giggle, a grand escape.

A leaf once flat, now wears a grin,
"It's great to be bright!" it sings within.
The clap of wind, a funny dance,
Whispers secrets, like a mischievous romance.

Fungi poke fun, their shapes so bizarre,
Mushroom parties under a star.
Digging in dirt with a curious snout,
Worms' silly squiggles make us shout!

Join in the fun, the earth's great jest,
Nature's humor brings out our best.
In every shade, a chuckle will rise,
A tickle of joy beneath bright skies.

Beneath the Glistening Boughs

Under boughs where shadows dance,
Squirrels play tug-of-war at first glance.
With acorns as prizes, they play their game,
In the forest of giggles, nothing's the same.

The sun cascades through branches so fine,
Painting the world like cheap cheap wine.
Every rustle brings a chuckle or two,
As critters conspire in a leafy review.

A chubby raccoon with a pie in its paws,
Proclaims, "I'm the chef, and these are my flaws!"
Beneath glistening boughs, merriment resounds,
While nature's misfits dance all around.

Here in the woods, we all wear a grin,
As laughter and joy keep flowing within.
A playful breeze, nature's whimsical shroud,
Under glistening boughs, happiness loud!

The Art of Nature's Revival

Nature's canvas, a masterpiece bright,
Sprouting up giggles, in morning light.
A sunbeam brushes the flowers' cheek,
Each bloom grinning, so unique!

A bumblebee trips on a daisy's crown,
Spinning around, then falling down.
"Oops!" it buzzes, with a dizzy delight,
As the wind whispers, "You'll be alright."

Trees stand tall, telling tales of yore,
While branches sway, clapping for more.
The art of revival with colors that tease,
Bringing smiles on the soft summer breeze.

So let us rejoice in this vibrant stage,
Where nature acts out, page after page.
In every petal and seed that we see,
There's humor and healing, wild and free!

Veils of Vitality

In a garden dressed in green,
Whispers dance and play unseen.
A salad here can fix your day,
Toss the worries far away.

With every crunch, a giggle swells,
Nature's magic, who can tell?
A bite of spinach, feel the cheer,
Spinach smoothies, sip with glee, my dear!

Fruits with laughter, bright and bold,
Grapes that jingle, stories told.
Carrots wearing tiny hats,
Funny how they smile like cats!

In this realm of whimsy greens,
Every salad's fit for queens.
So toss your cares and let them roll,
Nature's humor—good for the soul!

The Alchemy of Foliage

Beneath the trees, the joke's on us,
A leaf may giggle, oh what a fuss!
When the breeze tickles with glee,
Nature's laughter sets us free.

The bushes shuffle, dance a bit,
With vines that giggle, life is lit!
Herbs trade puns with playful ease,
Rolling on the ground, if you please!

Mismatched colors, wild and bright,
A rainbow blooms, what a sight!
Each lilac wink, each rose's blush,
Nature's jesters in a rush.

So gather round for leafy fun,
When nature laughs, we've truly won!
With every herb, a bashful grin,
In this green world, let joy begin!

Secrets of the Verdant World

In the forest, secrets hide,
Mossy chortles slip and slide.
The ferns conspire, plotting schemes,
A leafy prank? It's better than dreams!

A dandelion, with a winking face,
Says, "Blow me now, let's win this race!"
A field of giggles, playful sprouts,
In this green zone, there's no doubts!

Tomatoes wear their spots with pride,
In the patch, we all reside!
With every sprout, a chuckle grows,
Nature's comedy—everyone knows!

So wander wild, and take a look,
Each green corner hides a book.
Open pages, hear them squeal,
In the zany world of nature's zeal!

Rebirth in the Thicket

In the thicket, tales unwind,
A berry bush, a joke to find.
A raspberry giggles, 'come take a bite!'
Who knew fruits could be so bright?

The twigs wear hats of silly fun,
While flowers dance, one by one.
A clover laughs when it's approached,
Says, "Pick me, friend, I'm just encroached!"

The wild weeds offer riddles for moles,
With every twist, they play their roles.
Through sunlight streams and shadows deep,
Nature's secrets make us leap!

So in this thicket, wild and free,
Join the merriment, come and see!
With every step, a stifled cheer,
Nature's giggles draw us near!

Embraced by Green

In the garden, a plant does dance,
It tickles my nose, oh what a chance!
With every breeze, it sways and bends,
Making me laugh with all its friends.

A cabbage in shorts, looking quite dapper,
With a radish who can't stop its chortle and caper.
Together they jive, in a veggie parade,
Creating a ruckus, as laughter cascades.

The spinach wears shades, feeling quite cool,
While broccoli busts moves, breaking the rule.
Peas hold a party, as laughter erupts,
This green crowd knows how to lighten up!

As sunbeams shine down on this comical scene,
These funny green pals spread joy, so serene.
So let's join the laughter, don't sit on the fence,
With vegetables dancing, how can we be tense?

Green Caresses

A fern gives hugs, what a gentle sight,
Swaying along like it's holding you tight.
With each soft leaf, it whispers and sighs,
Sometimes even winking with goofy good eyes.

The grass has jokes tucked deep in its blades,
While flowers chuckle in vibrant cascades.
Each petal a laugh, blooming brilliant and bold,
In this leafy haven, not a single soul cold.

A cucumber slips and gives an 'oops' cheer,
As carrots giggle when they wipe their tears.
Underneath the sun's golden playful beam,
Nature brings humor; it's all just a dream.

So prance through the garden, and join in the fun,
With plant pals beside you, your laughter's begun.
Forget all your worries, let green spirits sing,
Amidst all this joy, the heart takes to wing.

Nature's Gentle Whisper

The willow bends low with a cheeky grin,
Tickling the toes of the ants passing in.
Each whisper from nature, a giggle so sweet,
While daisies fashion shoes made of wheat!

A mischievous breeze has a playful aim,
Twirling the leaves in a whimsical game.
They twirl and they spin, in a dance of delight,
Nature's laughter echoing into the night.

"Hey, up here!" cries a cheeky sunflower,
Covering its eyes, it shouts, "What a power!"
With bees buzzing choruses of silly tunes,
The gardens rejoice under giggling moons.

So take a deep breath of this giggling air,
With trees as your buddies, let laughter declare.
For nature's a jester, a whimsical sage,
In the book of the green, we turn a new page.

The Serenade of Sprouts

Oh, tiny sprouts with your bold little dreams,
Singing sweet tunes, or so it seems.
With a wiggle and jiggle, they sprout into view,
A concert of green, a delightful crew!

Leeks in tuxedos, marching in line,
While beets blushing red say, "This show's divine!"
Chard joins the chorus with its leafy flair,
They dance and they twirl without any care.

The radishes shout, "We're the stars of the night!"
While zucchini struts, feeling bold and bright.
The peas all chime in, with giggles galore,
Creating a symphony, inviting us for more.

So come join the concert, don't miss out,
With laughter so hearty, you'll surely shout.
This serenade of sprouts, such a merry delight,
In a world filled with giggles, life feels just right.

A Journey through Verdancy

Upon a leafy path we tread,
With twigs and laughs from nature spread.
The bushes chuckle, shadows dance,
We trip on roots, embrace our chance.

Frogs leap like they own the show,
Waving with tongues, 'Hello, amigo!'
A butterfly meets a beetle's grin,
'Hope we don't slip on that leaf again!'

Bumbling bees can't find their hives,
While other bugs are crafting jives.
A squirrel jokes with a gloomy crow,
'Why so blue? Just let it go!'

What fun we find in nature's cheer,
A giggle hidden so very near.
In this verdant world, let's frolic and roll,
Together we find that happiness is whole.

Roots of Rebirth

In the soil where laughter sprouts,
Tiny critters hold silly bouts.
A worm in a top hat shimmies around,
Tickling noses, spreading joy unbound.

Silly shadows from sunlit trees,
Dancing footprints in the gentle breeze.
A chipmunk with shades struts down the lane,
Sings 'I'm cooler than a soft summer rain!'

Roots dig deep, but only for fun,
They gather around, watch the jokes run.
A snail looks up, shrugs with a grin,
'Hey, at least we're not stuck in a tin!'

In muddy puddles they splash and they swish,
Every drop tastes like a silly wish.
Together they sprout and laugh with glee,
In this patch of life, let's be carefree.

The Calm Between Stems

In the quiet of foliage, whispers ignite,
Where tiny ants host a comical fight.
With acorns as helmets and laughs in the air,
They joust on the grass, without a care.

A toad on a leaf sings off-key,
While crickets jump up, 'Hey, that's me!'
The shadows grow long, the giggles increase,
They promise to share their silly feast.

Within this calm, a breeze finds its flow,
Tickling the ferns as they sway to and fro.
A deer winks softly at a flustered fox,
'Just try to outrun these silly rocks!'

In whispers and chuckles, the calm is alive,
Where laughter's the magic that helps us survive.
Here in the greens, with jokes on display,
We find our fun in the finest bouquet.

Nature's Anointed Calm

Amidst the green where spirits play,
Nature winks at us in a quirky way.
A lily laughs, 'This pond's my throne!'
While dragonflies buzz, 'We're never alone!'

In the garden of giggles, petals unfold,
Each petal a story, each story retold.
A daisy says, 'Together we shine!'
While the sun chuckles, 'You're all divine!'

The brook gurgles tales, bubbling bright,
Making bubbles that dance in the sunlight.
A bear joins in with a jolly song,
'This is the place where we all belong!'

And as the day wraps in nature's balm,
We gather the laughter, pour it like calm.
In this merry glade, we roots intertwine,
With chuckles and joy, forever we shine.

The Harmony of Herbal Hands

In the garden where the mint grows,
Laughter bubbles, comically it flows.
A sneeze from thyme, a tickling breeze,
The herbs conspire, putting minds at ease.

Oregano whispers jokes of the day,
Basil winks, showing off its sway.
Chives giggle, their humor so sharp,
Nature's laughter plays a merry harp.

Parsley struts with a jaunty flair,
Sage grins wide, without a care.
With every pluck, a pun is born,
In the herbal haven, we're never forlorn.

So come and join this leafy jest,
Where every herb is at its best.
A sprinkle of mirth, a dash of delight,
In the harmony of herbal delight.

Fronds of Forgiveness

In a forest where the ferns reside,
Whispers of peace and puns coincide.
A frond trips lightly, scaring a hare,
No need to fret, it just wanted to share.

Mossy carpets cushion the foulest of falls,
Crickets chuckle, ignoring the squalls.
Under the shade, secrets unfold,
While dandelions laugh, never too bold.

The vines entwine, sharing odd jokes,
Nature's comedians, dressed like folks.
Each giggle a breeze, each chuckle a shiver,
Forgiveness blooms like a magical river.

So dance in the grove, let humor unfold,
With fronds as friends, be brave and be bold.
For laughter and kindness lighten the load,
In this whimsical world, love's the true ode.

The Canopy's Comfort

Under the shade, where tall branches sway,
The canopy sings in a funny display.
Squirrels tell tales of the acorns they've lost,
While the wise old owl rolls eyes at the cost.

A gentle breeze carries giggles and grins,
While mossy cushions offer soft wins.
The sun peeks through, a playful tease,
Lighting up faces, putting us at ease.

Pine needles crackle, laughter like chimes,
Even the bark joins in with odd rhymes.
With every rustle, a chuckle is born,
In the cozy embrace of this leafy adorn.

So nestle in close, feel joy in the air,
The canopy's comfort, without a care.
With humor as the glue that binds us tight,
We share in the laughter from morning to night.

Canvas of the Woodland

In the woodland where art is alive,
Trees paint stories, where humor can thrive.
A cheeky chipmunk, with a brush in its paw,
Crafting a masterpiece that leaves us in awe.

The foliage giggles, each color a joke,
A canvas unfolds, with each quirky stroke.
Wildflowers dance, their petals a cheer,
While the bees laugh loudly, buzzing up near.

Bark chips are splashed with a dash of delight,
Nature's palette glows soft in the light.
With every layer, a chuckle will bloom,
In this joyous victory over the gloom.

So tip-toe through art where the wild things play,
In this whimsical gallery, we'll giggle away.
For every stroke told by nature's own hand,
Is a funny reminder — life's wonderfully planned.

The Whispering Woods

In the woods where laughter grows,
Trees giggle soft, in funny shows.
They tickle breezes, play tag with the air,
Funny faces hide everywhere.

Squirrels tell jokes, the owls hoot back,
Amid the rustle, there's never lack.
The mushrooms dance, so spry and spry,
While the pinecones wear a silly tie.

Caterpillars break into a dance,
While branches sway, they take a chance.
Nature's laughter, a merry swirl,
In the woods where joy unfurls.

So take a stroll, hear nature chime,
Where healing giggles stretch through time.
Leave your worries, let laughter steer,
In the whispering woods, good vibes are here!

Breathing with Botanicals

In a garden filled with glee,
Plants do yoga, just you see!
The roses stretch, in bright pink attire,
While daisies twirl, never tire.

Mint leaves snicker, 'We're the fresh crew!'
As sunflowers snap, 'We're due for a view!'
Thyme does a split, so spry and bold,
While the garlic just stands, looking old.

Cacti join in, with prickly flair,
"Breathe deeply," they shout, "We have time to spare!"
The thyme keeps time with a dainty beat,
While herbs take turns, showing their feet.

So join the dance, embrace the cheer,
With leafy friends, there's nothing to fear.
In breathing deep with botanical friends,
Health and laughter, the fun never ends!

The Healing Touch of Green

In gardens lush with shades of green,
Plants are comedians, if you know what I mean!
Kale cracks jokes while hiding in a patch,
And broccoli's style? Quite the catch!

The mint leaves gossip about last night's brew,
While the ferns share stories both funny and new.
Even the soil joins in on the fun,
Messy and fragrant, it knows how to run!

Grass blades whisper secrets so sly,
'Why did the corn get dizzy? Oh my!'
They roll on the ground, with laughter galore,
Stitching giggles in the earth evermore.

So step in the patch, let your heart gleam,
With the healing touch from nature's own dream.
Kick off those shoes, don't be shy or lean,
For laughter and love are the best and serene!

Renewal in the Grove

In the grove where giggles bloom,
Nature's punchlines fill the room.
The oak tree cracks jokes with a booming sound,
While the willows sway, wrapped in laughter profound.

The groundhog pokes his head out with flair,
"Is it spring yet? I need some fresh air!"
While the lilacs sashay, strutting around,
Twirling in breezes, they know they're renowned.

The acorns drop like tiny applause,
As squirrels engage in their nutty flaws.
Funny green friends, all sprightly and bright,
In the grove where day dances with night.

So come to the grove, let your spirit take flight,
In this whimsical place, everything feels right.
With renewal at hand and laughter in tow,
The joy of the green is a marvelous show!

www.ingramcontent.com/pod-product-compliance
Lightning Source LLC
Chambersburg PA
CBHW070314120526
44590CB00017B/2671